Ask a
PILOT

To my beautiful wife, who has supported me through this aviation adventure. And to my children and all other curious minds searching for answers. May they have clear skies and tailwinds. —J. K.

Published by Bushel & Peck Books, a family-run publishing house in Fresno, California, that believes in uplifting children with the highest standards of art, music, literature, and ideas. Find beautiful books for gifted young minds at www.bushelandpeckbooks.com.

Type set in Josefin Sans, Tomarik Brush, and Special Elite.

Design and illustration by David Miles.

Illustrations are mixed-media digital collages with elements sourced from public domain galleries or licensed from Shutterstock.com.
ILS gauge created by "Fred the Oyster," 2014.

Bushel & Peck Books is dedicated to fighting illiteracy all over the world. For every book we sell, we donate one to a child in need—book for book. To nominate a school or organization to receive free books, please visit www.bushelandpeckbooks.com.

LCCN: 2021944644
ISBN: 9781638190394

First Edition

Printed in the United States

10 9 8 7 6 5 4 3 2 1

Ask a PILOT

A Pilot Answers Kids' Questions About Air Travel

JUSTIN KELLEY

BUSHEL
& PECK
BOOKS

CONTENTS

INTRODUCTION

Do you dream of flying? If you answered yes, then this book is for you. On the other hand, if you answered no, and you started to sweat a little, and your heart started racing because the thought of trusting a huge, metal airplane that stays in the air by some unknown magic terrifies you, well . . . this book is also for you. *Especially* for you.

I am a pilot and I love teaching everyone about airplanes. I love talking about airplanes and airports and telling stories of my travels. Talking with people about flight has taught me something: When people are scared to go flying, it's usually because they don't understand what's going on. How does that airplane—something as big as a house—leave the ground? How does it float in the air like that? I've learned that once people understand what is happening, fear melts away.

In this book, you'll find answers to real questions from real kids. Some are funny, some are serious, but all them have real answers to help make flying a little less mysterious.

Let's begin at the airport with some of the most common questions I hear. Ready for takeoff? Here we go!

AT THE AIRPORT

1

WHERE DO THE BAGS GO?

Did you ever wonder why you can't take your luggage with you on the plane yourself? Or what happens to your bags after they go through that big hole in the wall behind the ticket counter?

Airplanes have only so much room. The area where people sit has enough room for only seats and a small storage area just big enough for everyone to bring one or two small bags. When you travel with a

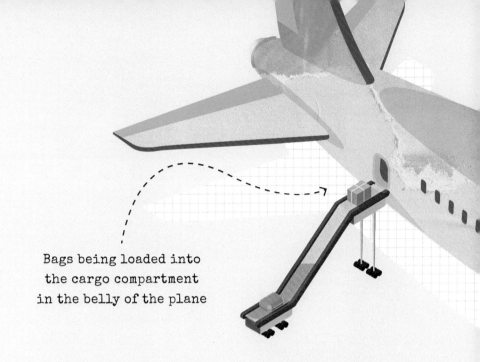

Bags being loaded into
the cargo compartment
in the belly of the plane

big bag, and almost everyone does, they
need to put that bag in a separate area
of the airplane made just for luggage.
This is usually a **cargo** area in the belly of
the plane.

May I take
your bag for
you?

Specially trained dogs can sniff out explosives and other dangerous items.

The path your bag travels from the counter to the airplane is fascinating! Underneath the airport and behind the walls is an entire city of conveyor belts, stairs, trucks, carts, and people working hard to make sure your bag gets to the right airplane.

When you give your bag to the people behind the counter, they put it on a conveyor belt that disappears behind a wall. Behind that wall, a network of more conveyor belts zooms your bag (and *lots* of other bags) to a large room where they'll be checked for knives, guns, and bombs. They do this using x-ray machines and dogs, and they will even open some of the bags and search them by hand!

After this big room, your bag goes on another series of conveyor belts until it ends up in a cart that will take it to your airplane. This cart will not be the only one, either. There will be several carts that they'll hook together like a train. If you are paying attention, you might see this train pulling up to your airplane.

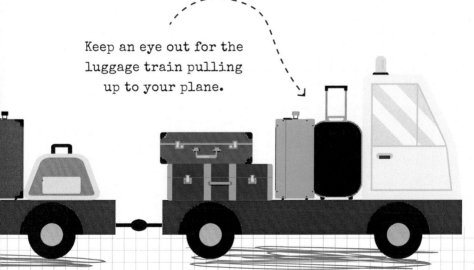

Keep an eye out for the luggage train pulling up to your plane.

2

WHY DO WE GO THROUGH SECURITY?

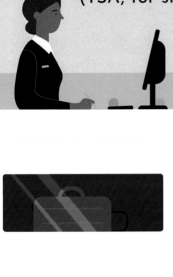

Airports work very hard to make sure that flights are safe. In the United States, that's the job of the Transportation Security Administration (TSA, for short). Other countries have

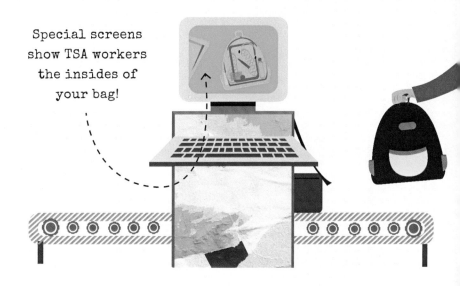

Special screens show TSA workers the insides of your bag!

their own agencies, but they all want to do the same thing: catch any possible bad guys before they get to an airplane. To do this, they must screen everyone—just to make sure. That is why you take off your jacket and your backpack and walk through those machines. The machines are specially designed to find things that might be dangerous, like bombs, knives, or guns. Every person, backpack, purse, and pair of shoes gets looked at one-by-one to make sure there's nothing hidden inside.

3

WHAT IF I GET LOST?

Your gate number

NAME OF PASSENGER
FLYE / I. WILL

FROM: CHICAGO
TO: FRESNO / FA

GATE
A47

ETKT 5552115239450

Airports are a big place! It's normal to feel a little concerned about all the crowds. To stay safe, the most important thing you can do is stick with your group. Are you traveling with family or with your school or club? Stay with them.

If you do get lost, find a grown-up in uniform who can help. They are everywhere and easy to find. They might be a ticket agent, a police officer, or even a pilot like me, and they will know how to help you find your group. They might ask what gate your group is going to. You can find the gate number on your ticket, also called a **boarding pass**. Printed right there on every

BOARDING PASS

ECONOMY

FLIGHT
OKL018

ECONOMY

SEAT
24A

NAME OF PASSENGER
FLYE / I. WILL

FROM: CHICAGO / ORD
TO: FRESNO / FAT

FLIGHT
OKL018

DATE

ARDING TIME
1:30

GATE
A47

BOARDING TIME
11:30

GATE CLOSES 40 MINUTES BEFORE DEPARTURE

ETKT 5552115239450

SEAT

HAVE A NICE TR

Air Company

ticket is a letter with a number. That will tell you which door your airplane is parked at.

The airport also has ways to make announcements over loudspeakers. This is another way they can quickly locate your group, so rest assured that you will find them again!

Above all, remember "stranger danger" rules. Never go anywhere you are alone with a stranger.

Beaumont le gagnant sur monoplan Blériot
moteur Gnôme, magnéto Bosch

ON THE
AIRPLANE

4

IS IT REALLY THAT IMPORTANT TO TURN EVERYTHING TO AIRPLANE MODE?

Yes, this is a very important rule. Airplanes are essentially flying computers with lots of electronics working together to help the pilots fly safely. All the passengers' mobile phones, tablets, and other devices have signals that could disrupt those electronics.

Most devices have a designated airplane mode to prevent them from interfering with the plane's electronics.

This is especially true when there are hundreds of these devices transmitting at once. So, the Federal Aviation Administration has created a law that says those devices need to be in airplane mode. Please obey it!

5

WHY IS IT SO BUMPY?

B umps don't happen all the time, but they sure can feel scary. This is called **turbulence**. Sometimes it feels like the seat drops away from beneath you and butterflies start fluttering in your stomach. But don't worry! In reality, the airplane probably hasn't moved up or down more than just a few feet. It might feel like more, but some of that is enhanced because of the nervousness that you feel. When you are scared, you focus on

Air ripples when it goes over uneven ground—like mountains— and causes turbulence.

what is scaring you, and if you fear flying, you are hyper-focused on every sensation.

So, why do those drops happen? It's actually quite simple. Have you ever been on a boat? Or maybe you have watched the ripples in the water while standing on the shore. Just like water, when air moves over uneven ground like mountains and valleys, it swirls and ripples. These ripples can be small or large, and sometimes they're big enough that you can feel them thousands of feet above the ground.

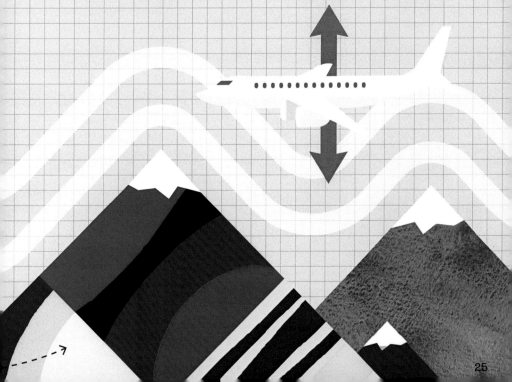

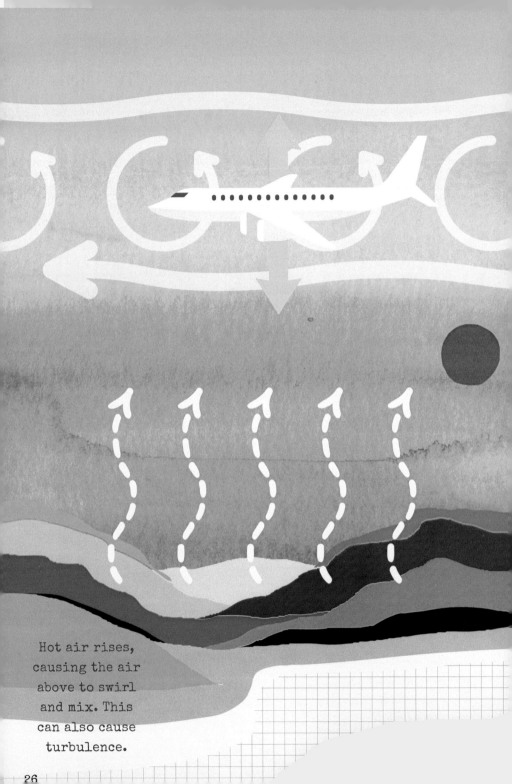

Hot air rises,
causing the air
above to swirl
and mix. This
can also cause
turbulence.

There are other reasons the air swirls and ripples. As the ground heats up from the sun, the air around the ground gets hot and rises into the cooler air above it. This causes the air to swirl and mix. There might also be wind from two different directions that meet and mix, causing other swirls.

Air is not stable or constant. Just like the surface of a lake or the ocean, air is in constant motion. As a boat moves across the water into the waves, it might bump and move, but it won't sink. An airplane is the same way. As it flies through the unstable air, it bumps and moves, but this is not dangerous—unless you are standing up. Even little bumps can make you fall. That is why we turn the seatbelt sign on.

6

I HEAR CHIMES. WHAT DO THEY MEAN?

As you relax on your flight, you might notice several bell sounds or chimes. These are not actual bells but are several *dings* that sound through the speakers at different times of the flight. Each sound means something different.

The easiest one to identify is the seat belt sound. Every time the pilots turn the seat belt sign on or off, there is a chime that plays. This is to make sure that you both see and hear that it is time to return to your seat or that you are free to use the restroom.

The other chimes you might hear are very similar and are mostly there to help the pilot communicate with the flight attendants on what phase of the flight they are in. These chimes might mean that the airplane has climbed past 10,000 feet, is cruising, that the descent has started, or that they are just a few minutes from landing. This helps flight attendants know when they can get up, make announcements, serve snacks, and collect trash.

The next time you hear the chimes, watch carefully and see what the flight attendants do.

7

ARE THUNDERSTORMS DANGEROUS?

The bad news is that yes, thunderstorms can be dangerous. Storms can cause turbulence (see page 24) that might be strong enough to injure passengers and crew. And though planes are designed to handle lightning strikes, there is always a chance that a strike in just the right spot could damage the plane's electrical systems.

Fortunately,
thunderstorms are
easy to see and go
around.

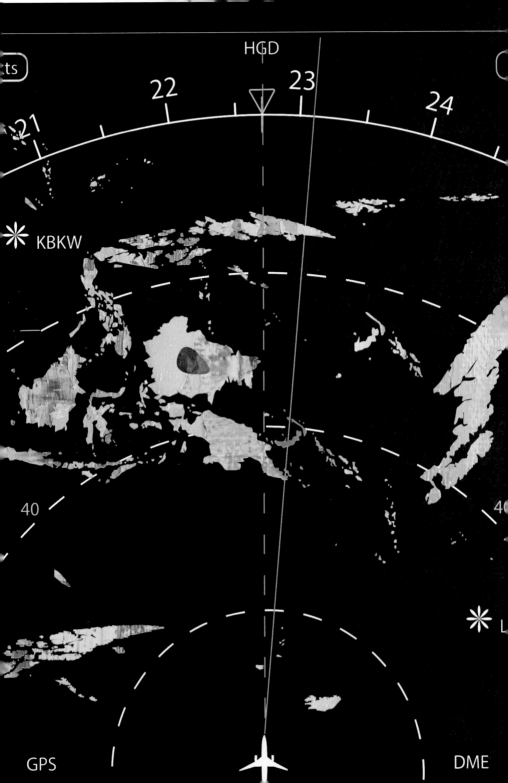

The good news, however, is that pilots have lots of training and practice to handle storms. Even better, storms are usually easy to see and avoid. The boiling clouds that climb high into the sky are the types that contain thunder and lightning. When we see these, we fly around them.

Sometimes, a storm might be surrounded by other clouds that are not dangerous but that hide the storm. We call these embedded thunderstorms. For these situations, we have radar and satellite imagery in the flight deck to help us see where these storms are so we can fly around them.

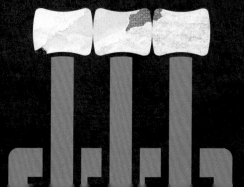

8

HOW DOES WIND AFFECT FLYING?

A lot! Winds can be very strong. Depending on the time of year and how high you are, you might experience wind that is several hundred miles per hour. In the air, this isn't a big deal; the only thing impacted is navigation. If I am trying to fly forward, for example, and the wind is blowing in from the right, then the airplane will be pushed left and I'll be off course. To stop this, I turn the airplane a little to the right of the direction I'm trying to fly. This keeps me flying where I want to go. The airplane still flies the same, and unless you were looking at the navigation instruments, you would never know how strong the winds were.

By steering slightly right into the wind, the plane continues to go straight.

Crabbing

Crosswind
landing

This all changes during take-off and landing, though. Imagine that a plane is trying to land on a runway while the wind is blowing in from the right. You might think that in order to fly a straight line to the runway, the airplane nose has to be pointed to the right of the runway. This is fine in the air, but if you're trying to land, this would mean that the airplane will come to the runway slightly sideways. This is called **crabbing**, and if the pilot tries to touch the wheels down on the runway while crabbing, he or she might damage the airplane. What the pilot needs to do instead is bring the nose back straight to the runway and then lower the right wing into the wind. This keeps the airplane flying straight to the runway and lines up the airplane for touchdown. This maneuver is called a **crosswind landing** and is something that pilots practice a lot.

9

Motion-
sickness
medicine can
really help.

WHAT IF
I GET SICK?

It's not fun to talk about, but getting sick on an airplane does happen. Fortunately, the crew is more than prepared to help you.

Before you fly, it might be a good idea to bring some ginger candy or some age-appropriate motion sickness medicine on the flight. If you still feel sick on the flight, then make sure to find a sickness bag. These are special bags that every airplane keeps in the back pocket of the seat in front of you. It's best to grab two if you can: one to use if you get sick, and another to keep as a quick backup. Be sure to hand the used bag to the flight attendants as soon as you can. One thing that they really do not like is finding used sick bags shoved back into the pocket of the seat.

A flight attendant can also help you turn on the air vent to blow cool air on your face. It helps! They might also give you a cool washcloth to hold on your forehead. Above all, they will be kind and sympathetic. Getting sick happens to lots of people—even me! (see page 98)—so don't feel embarrassed if it happens to you.

And please don't leave them in the pocket.

Be sure to grab two bags, just in case!

+

10

WHY DO MY EARS FEEL FUNNY?

If you have ever taken a deep breath and jumped into the pool as far down as you can go, you might have noticed that your ears feel funny, almost like the water is pushing and trying to get inside. This happens because the water has weight, and the deeper you are, the more water you have pushing down on you and your ears.

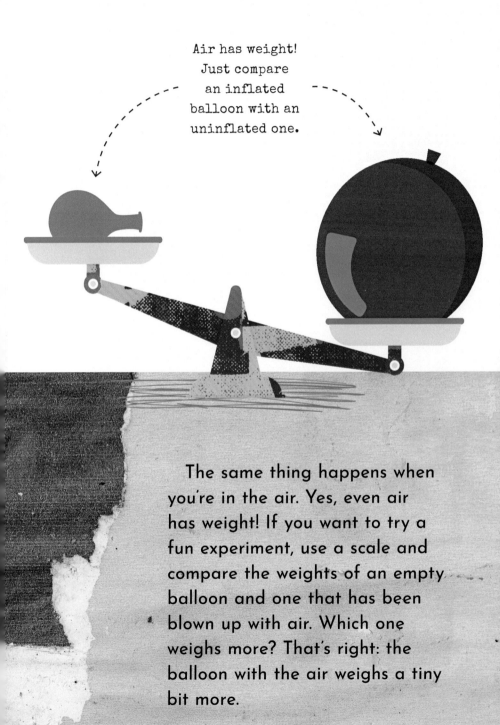

Air has weight!
Just compare
an inflated
balloon with an
uninflated one.

The same thing happens when you're in the air. Yes, even air has weight! If you want to try a fun experiment, use a scale and compare the weights of an empty balloon and one that has been blown up with air. Which one weighs more? That's right: the balloon with the air weighs a tiny bit more.

62 MILES OF AIR

Air doesn't weigh very much, but a lot of air does!

Even though air doesn't weigh very much, there's a lot of it weighing down on you. To get out of our **atmosphere**—to the end of the air— you would need to go sixty-two miles straight up. That means there is sixty-two-miles worth of air pushing down on you making pressure. Normally, you don't feel this because this pressure is constant and your body is really good at ignoring sensations that are constant. When you're in an airplane, however, you move up and down through the air, and the amount of air pressing down on you changes depending how high you are. When you go up, the pressure decreases. When you go down, the pressure increases.

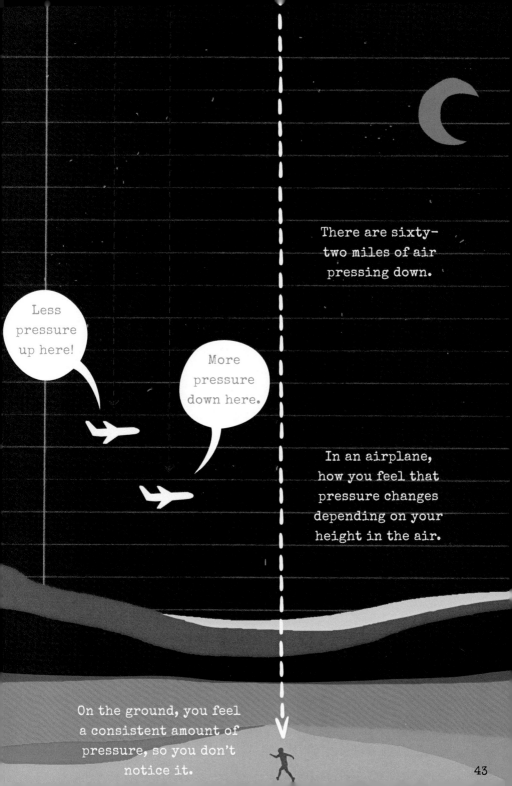

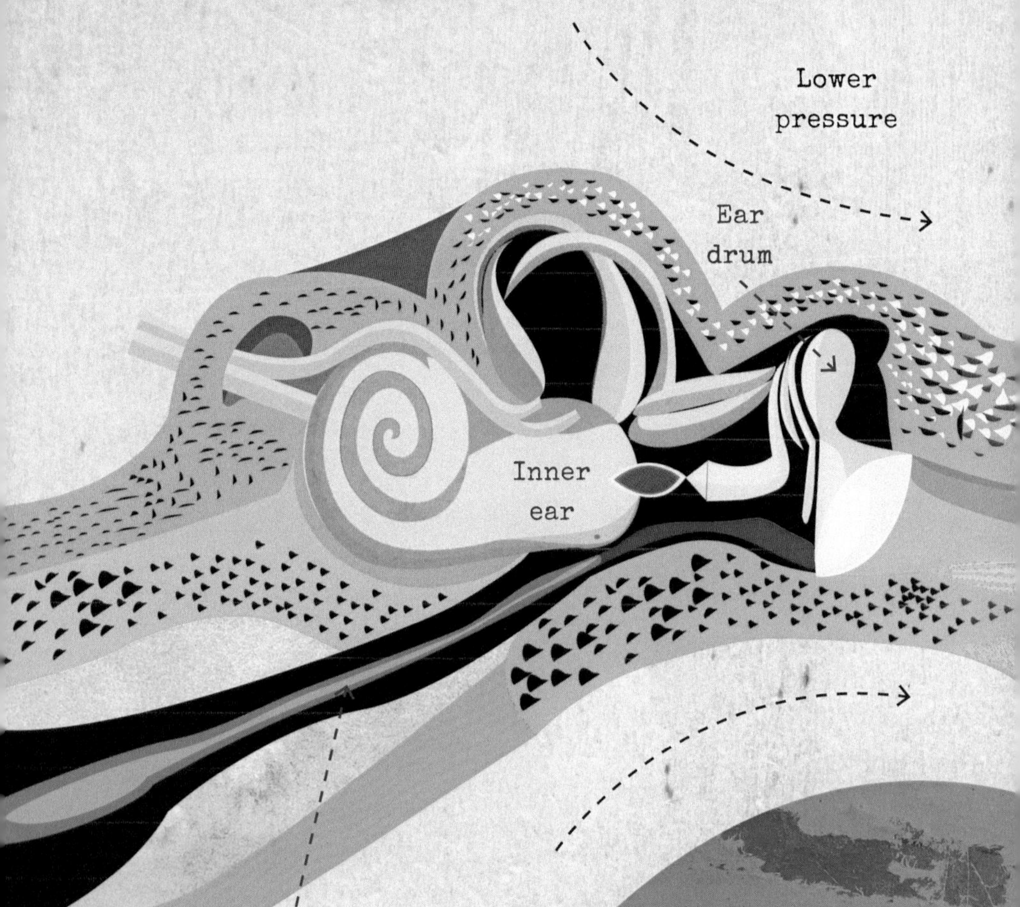

Lower
pressure

Ear
drum

Inner
ear

Eustachian
tube

Increasing
pressure is
what causes the
most discomfort for
people. This is because
the air outside the ear is
trying to equalize with the air
inside the ear by pushing in. This does
not work very well, as the pressure outside
causes the Eustachian tube of the ear to
collapse, preventing air from coming in

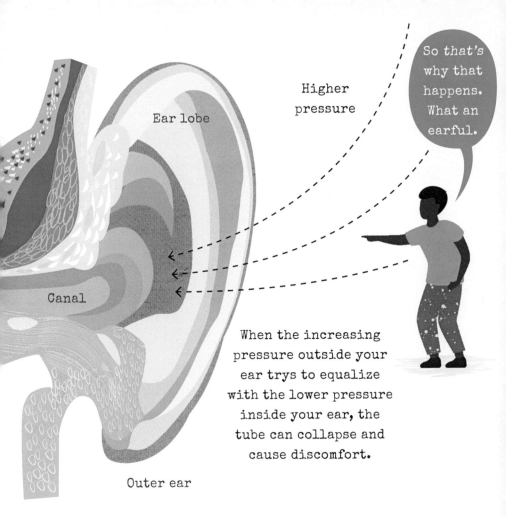

Ear lobe

Higher
pressure

So *that's*
why that
happens.
What an
earful.

Canal

When the increasing
pressure outside your
ear trys to equalize
with the lower pressure
inside your ear, the
tube can collapse and
cause discomfort.

Outer ear

and making the difference in pressure even
worse. To relieve the pressure, hold your
nose and close your mouth. While doing this,
"blow" while not letting any air out of your
nose or mouth. This will force the air inside
your ears out through the tubes, opening
them up and equalizing the inside of your
ear with the air outside. This is known as
"popping" your ears, and it's such a relief!

Making all this just a tiny bit more complicated, airliners also come with machinery that works to **pressurize** the cabin. A computer-controlled pump and series of valves cause the air to increase and decrease in pressure as the plane moves. This is necessary because airliners fly high enough that the air is too thin to breath. If we did not have pressurization, we would all pass out from lack of air. The moment the airplane first lifts off the runway, the pumps start pressurizing the cabin to keep it feeling similar to how you feel on the ground. But because the body of the aircraft can only handle so much of a pressure difference between the inside of the cabin and the outside air, the pumps don't perfectly match ground levels.

CABIN PRESSURE

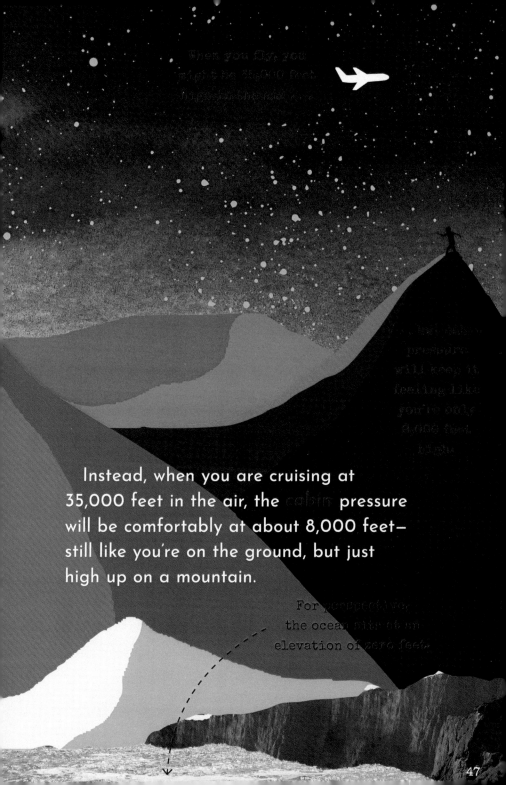

When you fly, you might be 35,000 feet high in the air... you...

Your cabin pressure will keep it feeling like you're only 8,000 feet high.

Instead, when you are cruising at 35,000 feet in the air, the cabin pressure will be comfortably at about 8,000 feet— still like you're on the ground, but just high up on a mountain.

For perspective, the ocean sits at an elevation of zero feet.

The computer starts pressurizing the aircraft as soon as the wheels leave the ground. This might cause your ears to feel like they need to be popped even though you are climbing because the cabin is increasing in pressure. After this initial pressurization, your ears should feel fine for the rest of the climb and cruise.

As the airplane descends closer to the ground at the end of the flight, the cabin once again starts to pressurize so that the outside pressure and inside pressure will match as the wheels touch down on the runway. As you get closer to the ground, you'll need to pop your ears multiple times.

TAKE-OFF:

Cabin pressurization begins to keep the cabin comfortable at high altitudes.

LANDING:

Cabin pressurization happens again to acclimate paassengers' bodies to normal, surface-level air pressure.

11

Those really are tiny.

WHY ARE THE WINDOWS SO TINY?

Small airplanes that stay low to the ground can have large windows. But large airliners, like the ones you'll usually fly on, fly very high and very fast and have to be pressurized (see "Why do my ears feel funny?" on page 40).

The body of an airliner—also called the **fuselage**—is built tough with zero leaks for air to escape. Windows make that much more difficult to control. In fact, the whole system would work much

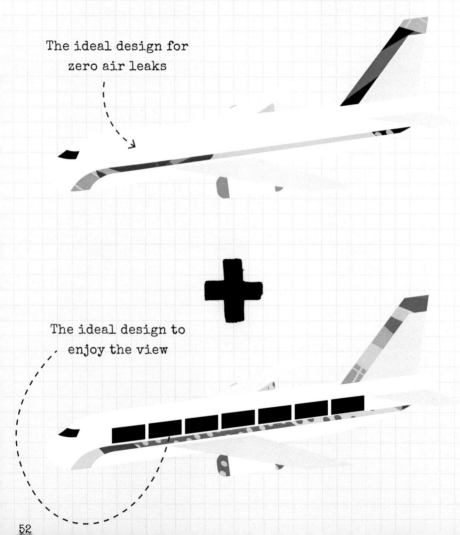

The ideal design for zero air leaks

The ideal design to enjoy the view

better with no windows! (This is one reason cargo airplanes don't have them.) But airline companies know that people like to look out at the world below them, so they made a compromise: they allow windows to be installed, but they restrict the number and size so that it is easier to pressurize the airplane.

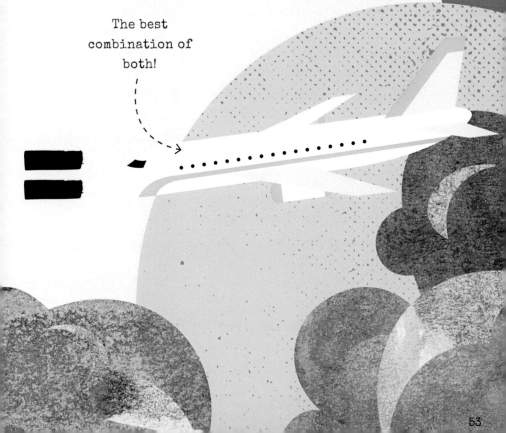

The best combination of both!

12

CAN AIRPLANES LAND IN FOG?

Yes and no. The answer to this question really depends on the aircraft you are flying and on the runway you are trying to land on. In the case of bad fog, there are procedures called instrument approaches that can guide pilots to runways that they can't physically see. These procedures use **GPS** or radio signals, but not all are created equal. Some will guide the pilot closer to the runway than others. If the pilot cannot see the runway by the lowest **altitude** on the approach, then he or she must climb away from the airport and try something else (or fly to another airport).

The most accurate of these approaches is called the **Instrument Landing**

Procedure, or ILS for short. The most basic ILS is the CAT I, and this can guide the airplane to within two-hundred feet off the ground and within half a mile of the runway. CAT II will get you even closer, and CAT III will bring you to within just fifty feet above the end of the runway! All these approaches require special equipment on the airplane and at the airport to work.

Beaumont le gagnant sur monoplan Blériot
moteur Gnome, magneto Bosch

FLIGHT

ADMIT ONE
09871234
09871234

HOW
AIRPLANES
WORK

13

Everyone think happy thoughts!

HOW DO THOSE BIG, HEAVY AIRPLANES LEAVE THE GROUND?

et's play a game. Close your eyes and pretend you are riding in a car going down the highway. Open the window and stick out your hand. What do you feel? Wind! And a lot of it.

Now here's a question: If you make your hand completely flat with the palm facing down towards the street, how hard is the wind pushing your hand? Not very much; in fact, it probably feels like your hand is slicing through the air.

Wind

Now put your palm forward facing the same direction the car is moving. How much wind do you feel now? A lot more, and probably like the wind is pushing your hand back. If it feels like you are fighting with the wind, this is because you are.

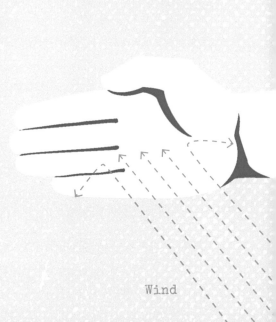

Wind

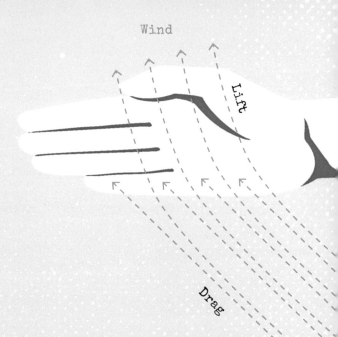

Wind

Lift

Drag

Now, see what happens if you tilt your hand at an angle in between the first two positions. Do you feel your hand raise up on its own? This is the wind trying to push your hand both back and up. The up push you feel is called **lift**. The backward push is called **drag**.

You might be thinking, "Sure it pushes hard, but it's not enough to make an *airplane* fly." But imagine that your hand is bigger. A lot bigger. The size of a semi-truck! And imagine the car is going a *lot* faster. How hard do you think the wind is pushing on your hand now?

That's the secret of flight. For an airplane to leave the ground, it needs strong engines to push it through the air, strong wings for the wind to push back, and presto! You leave the earth behind.

61

Over the years, engineers have developed lots of different wings with slightly different shapes that have a huge impact on how the wings interact with the wind. We call these shapes **airfoils**. For airfoils to work, they need air rushing past, just like your hand out of the car window. This is done by moving the airplane forward at high speeds with propellors or jet engines. When the wing is shaped just right, the force pushing up will be greater than the force pushing down, and the airplane will rise into the air.

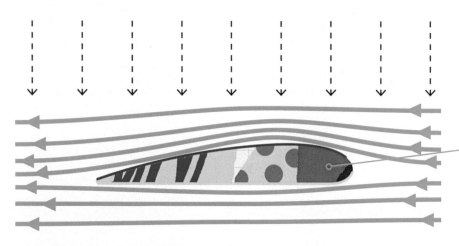

The air rushing below the wing moves faster than the air moving above the wing, resulting in more force pushing up than pushing down.

Speaking of force, there are four main forces that act on an airplane in flight:

GRAVITY is the force that fights against lift and tries to keep the airplane on the ground.

DRAG is the force created by air pushing against the airplane as it moves through the air.

LIFT is the force generated by the wings lifting the aircraft into the air.

THRUST is the force created by the engines that pulls the airplane through the air.

Achieving flight is a simple balancing act with all four of these forces. If you want to **climb**, then you need enough force to push through the air and create enough lift to overcome gravity. If you want to level off, then you simply need to decrease the lift just a little so that it equals gravity rather than overcomes it. Need to **descend**? Decrease the lift a little more. The more lift you take away, the faster you will descend. Adjusting thrust and drag will change how fast you travel altogether.

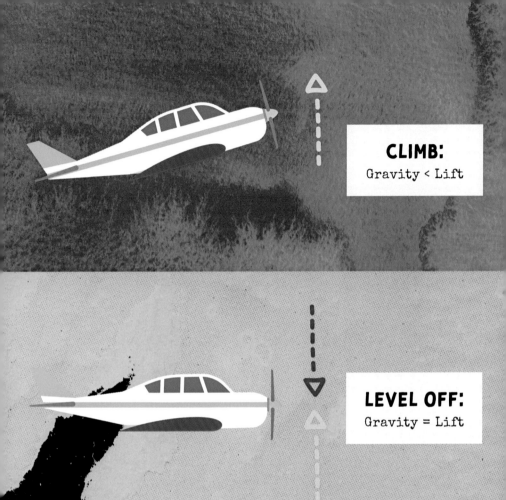

CLIMB:
Gravity < Lift

LEVEL OFF:
Gravity = Lift

DESCEND:
Gravity > Lift

14

Tag, you're it!

WHY DON'T AIRPLANES RUN INTO EACH OTHER?

A lot of time, training, and technology has gone into the practices we have today to avoid mid-air collisions. There are three main systems in place that prevent these types of accidents: the pilots, air traffic control, and traffic avoidance systems.

THE PILOTS: From our very first flight lesson, pilots are taught to look for and avoid other aircraft. There are specific procedures we all follow when dealing with airports and runways. Traffic patterns are mostly standardized and there are rules that say which airplane gets to go first.

"Driving" a plane at an airport is just like driving a car anywhere else: there are rules about when to turn and who goes first.

AIR TRAFFIC CONTROL: When lots of airplanes are in busy airspace together, **air traffic control** is extremely important. Through radio, pilots receive specific instructions that need to be followed regarding our **course**, altitude, and speed. We also listen to the other aircraft and do our best to develop a mental picture of what all the other airplanes around us are doing.

Maneuvering to steer clear of another airplane is something all pilots are trained to do, but is something they should never *have* to do. The safest way to avoid other aircraft is to never be close to them in the first place.

TRAFFIC AVOIDANCE SYSTEMS: There are also traffic avoidance systems; specifically, there is the **traffic collision avoidance system** (TCAS). The TCAS system allows computers of different aircraft to talk to each other and share information on course, altitude, and speed. If two airliners are on course to collide, the system will warn the pilots and give them guidance on how to maneuver away from the other aircraft.

Go up!

This is considered an emergency procedure. If this ever has to happen, then something else has already gone wrong and reports must be filed so the Federal Aviation Administration can review the data and figure out if any policy change needs to take place.

Go down!

15

HOW WIDE ARE AIRPLANE WINGS?

Wings need to be specially designed for the needs of the aircraft that will use them. Will the airplane cross oceans with three-hundred passengers and weigh over 900,000 pounds, or is it only going to fly for a few hours around the local area with two or three people? Just like some airplanes are made to go fast and do flips while some are not, some are really good at carrying lots of weight and flying high while others are just fun to buzz around the local sky.

When it comes to wings, here are a few general rules. If you want to have an aircraft fly fast and do loops and super-tight turns, then the wings need to be short and stubby. If you want the airplane to fly efficiently over long distances at really high altitudes, then the wings need to be longer and skinnier. For jets that fly high and near the speed of sound, the wings need to be *very* long and skinny and sweep backwards towards the tail.

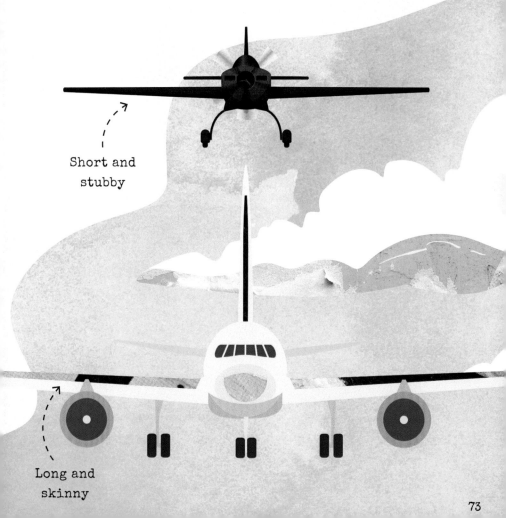

Short and
stubby

Long and
skinny

16

HOW FAST ARE AIRPLANES?

There are as many different types of airplanes as there are cars, motorcycles, trucks, and buses. When you first start flying, you fly small, slow airplanes. This is a good thing; small airplanes are easier to fly, and the slower you go, the more time you have to think through the flight. Pilots like to "stay ahead of the airplane," which means being able to plan for what is going to happen *before* it happens. After all, you can't pull an airplane over to the side of the road!

Light aircraft
188 mph

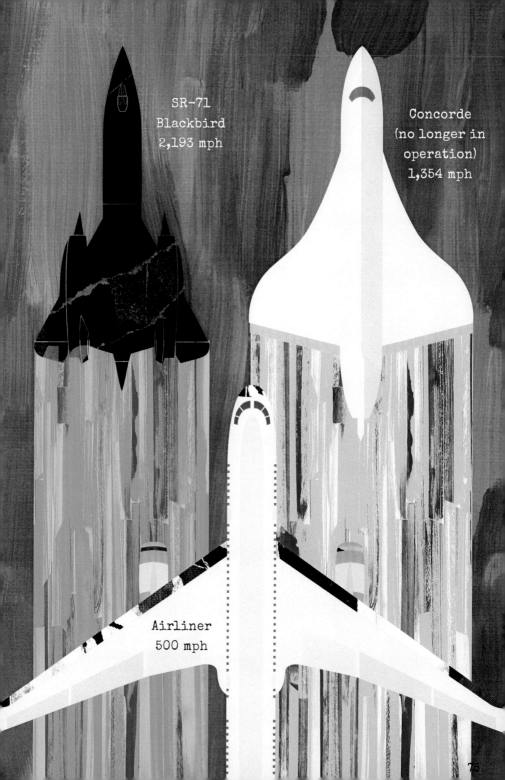

SR-71
Blackbird
2,193 mph

Concorde
(no longer in
operation)
1,354 mph

Airliner
500 mph

As an airline pilot, I fly fast—about 500 miles per hour, which means I could fly from New York City to North Carolina in just one hour (as opposed to *eight* hours if driving by car). But there are a lot of airplanes that can fly faster. The fastest airplane ever built was the SR-71 Blackbird. This was a military spy jet that could fly over 2,000 miles per hour! That is so fast

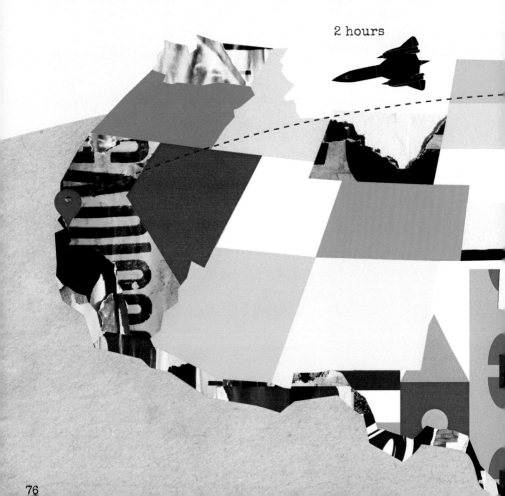

2 hours

that you could fly from New York City all the way to San Francisco in just a couple of hours.

Sometimes, if you're flying at a low altitude, you might feel like you're flying super fast even if your speed isn't actually that high. Race airplanes, for example, will fly only 200-400 miles an hour when less than 100 feet off the ground. But at these speeds and at that low to the ground, the world is truly a blur!

1 hour

17

WHY ARE THERE SO MANY BUTTONS WHEN THE AIRPLANE DOES ONLY ONE THING?

Do airplanes *really* do only one thing? The answer is no, of course; they do lots of things! Sure, the main thing they do is fly from one airport to the next. But think of all the things that have to happen to do that. To fly, you need an engine—and airliners usually have more than one. Each engine needs controls for starting, running, adding and removing power, and shutting down.

There are lots of buttons because airplanes do lots of things!

An airplane also has flight controls. These controls allow for **banking**, turning, climbing, and descending, and they're managed with hydraulics and electricity. That means that there have to be controls for the those hydraulics, generators, batteries, and circuits. There are also landing gear, brakes, air conditioning, pressurization, systems that help melt ice buildup on the outside, and navigation in the form of GPS and radio. So really, an airplane does hundreds of things! And that is why there are hundreds of little buttons and switches.

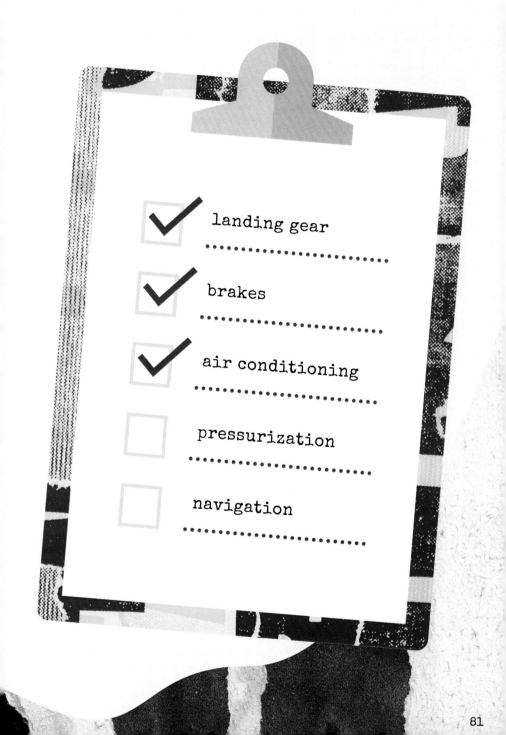

- ✓ landing gear
- ✓ brakes
- ✓ air conditioning
- ☐ pressurization
- ☐ navigation

18

CAN YOU LAND IN THE MIDDLE OF NOWHERE?

This completely depends on the airplane. Just like some cars need nice, flat pavement, and some cars can go bouncing down rocky riverbeds, airplanes are built to do different things. Airliners like the ones you'll most likely fly on need very specific landing surfaces. These are big, heavy planes that need to go

very fast down a smooth runway to get off the ground. Having an uneven surface would most likely break the wheels.

A plane's design might limit the places you can physically land, but you might be surprised to learn that there are very few limitations on where you can *legally* land. There are laws, of course, about staying certain distances away from large groups of people and away from private property, but most of the land in the United States is open land. There are many pilots who like to take special airplanes specifically designed to land on rough terrain and go land in the middle of nowhere on all sorts of mountains, valleys, and riverbeds.

BEING A
PILOT

19

WHY ARE THERE TWO PILOTS WHEN JUST ONE COULD CONTROL THE PLANE?

wo heads are better than one! Have you ever worked on a class project where someone else helped you see a problem in a way you hadn't thought of before? Flying needs good problem-solving, too, and it's best to have people who can work together to do that.

Good thinking.

On each airliner, there is a **captain** and a **first officer**. But even though they're called different things, both are real pilots, both have lots of experience and knowledge, and both are completely qualified to operate the aircraft safely. In fact, before you can even get hired by an airline in the United States, you must have had at least 1,500 hours of

time in the air being a pilot (that would be like flying an airplane for two whole months without any breaks to eat or sleep!).

Before I was hired for my first airline job as a first officer, I had actually already been a captain at a charter company. So rest assured that the captain and first officer on your next flight have all the experience they need.

Back in the early days of airline flying—way back in the 1950s and 1960s—there was a real sense of rank among **crew members** on an airplane. Whatever the captain said carried ultimate authority and was rarely questioned. But during the 1970s and 1980s, there were several high-profile accidents that happened when captains made bad decisions. They were good captains and good pilots with lots of experience, but they were also human—and humans can make mistakes. The real problem was that in each of those accidents, most of the first officers disagreed with the decisions the captains made and felt there was a better way, but they were afraid to speak up.

Today, captains and crew members are trained differently. Every pilot in the flight deck is a valued crew member and is supposed to speak up with their concerns and solutions to all problems that might arise with a flight. The captain still has ultimate authority, but the first officer is encouraged—and even expected—to question decisions they do not understand. Captains are expected to use and depend on the knowledge of the first officer as a very real and valid resource.

There are, of course, other reasons why having two pilots is a good idea. There are two roles in the flight deck: pilot flying and pilot monitoring. One pilot flies the airplane while the other pilot monitors the actions and the decisions of the pilot flying. The pilot monitoring also handles all the radio calls and manages the systems so the pilot flying can focus on that one very important job. The captain makes the decision as to who fills what role and how often, but the common practice is that the pilots switch roles every other flight.

CAPTAIN
The captain has senior authority, often sits in the left chair, and can be identified by his four stripes.

CHIEF PURSER
The chief purser is the senior flight attendant and is responsible for all other attendants and operations.

FIRST OFFICER
The first officer usually sits in the right chair, has three stripes, and is a fully qualified pilot.

20

HAVE YOU EVER CRASHED?

Thankfully, no! Although that really depends on your definition of "crash." I have had several emergency situations where the aircraft was safely navigated to the ground, and I have had situations that left the aircraft slightly damaged. But I was never in any kind of accident that I think most would consider a crash.

One day, I was flying a small, four-passenger airplane. This airplane had two small engines and was mainly used for training newer pilots. On this particular day, I was out flying just for fun. As I was descending into the valley of Truckee, California, I looked to my right to try to spot another aircraft that was landing at the same airport. But as I did, I noticed

my wing tip had a huge gaping hole
in it! I was more surprised than scared.
The main part of the wing was fine, and
the airplane was still flying great. It was
confusing, though, because I couldn't
remember having hit anything or having
anything strike *me* that could have caused
the damage. After I landed, I bought

some aircraft-specific tape from the local airplane mechanics and taped up the hole before returning home where the regular mechanic could properly fix the airplane.

Another time, I was coming in for a landing and had a flat tire. This ended up fine, but it's one of those situations that, if not handled correctly, could easily have ended up worse. I was in that same, small, two-engine airplane as before, again out for some fun flying. My **touchdown** on the runway was nice and the initial rollout was fine. After a few seconds, though, I felt the aircraft suddenly lean to the right and start to turn towards the edge of the runway. I quickly tried to steer the airplane back

to the left, but I only managed
to slow it down. The edge of the
runway was coming closer, and at
this point, all I could do was try
to stop the aircraft as quickly
as I could. Fortunately, I was
able to before the plane slid
off the runway, and nothing
was broken on the airplane
except the flat tire.

21

HOW OFTEN DO YOU FLY?

If you love flying as much as I do, the answer is: not enough! Airline pilots' schedules are constantly changing. You can fly anything from one day at a time to four days straight, staying in a different hotel every night. You might fly one flight in a day, or you might fly four or five flights.

(This can be very tiring, and by the end, you feel a little beat up. All you can think about is getting off that airplane!) If you work several days in a row, then you typically have several days off, so it works out.

Some pilots are on **reserve**. This means that they are not working any flight but are required to be close to the airport in case they're called in to replace another pilot who is unable to do the flights he or she was assigned. A typical pilot will work just over half the month. Flying can sometimes be tiring and even tedious, but on the whole, I sure love doing it for my work!

22

HAVE YOU EVER GOTTEN SICK?

Yes, even pilots get sick! As a child, I used to get carsick. When I first started flight training, I would start to feel ill if the lesson was too long or if we were doing certain maneuvers.

One of the first, more intense maneuvers you learn is what pilots call a **steep turn**. With this turn, you bank the wings at forty-five degrees and turn in a tight circle. The turn is fast, and the small aircraft you are training in will turn 360 degrees in just a few seconds. When I was first training this move, I would often get sick.

Fortunately, getting sick as a pilot is more mental than physical. It usually happens because your mind gets confused about what "up" and "down" should be.

When the balance you feel inside doesn't match what your eyes see outside, you start to feel sick. But, because it is mostly in your mind, you can learn to train your body to handle the experience. I no longer get sick on any airplanes and I can do all sorts of maneuvers. As a bonus, I don't get carsick anymore, either. I can even read in the car, and I was never able to do that until after I learned to fly!

For a pilot, getting sick is more mental than physical.

23

DO YOU GET TO LISTEN TO MUSIC WITH THOSE HEADPHONES?

No. In fact, the whole reason we have those headphones is that airplanes can be loud. There is a lot of communication that happens over the radio and between the two pilots, and the headphones make it easier to hear each other over the noise of the plane. From the time we push back from the **gate** to the time we park at the next airport, pilots are in constant contact with air traffic controllers. These controllers are split up with different responsibilities and we often need to monitor multiple **frequencies** throughout the flight. There are controllers

Roger
that.

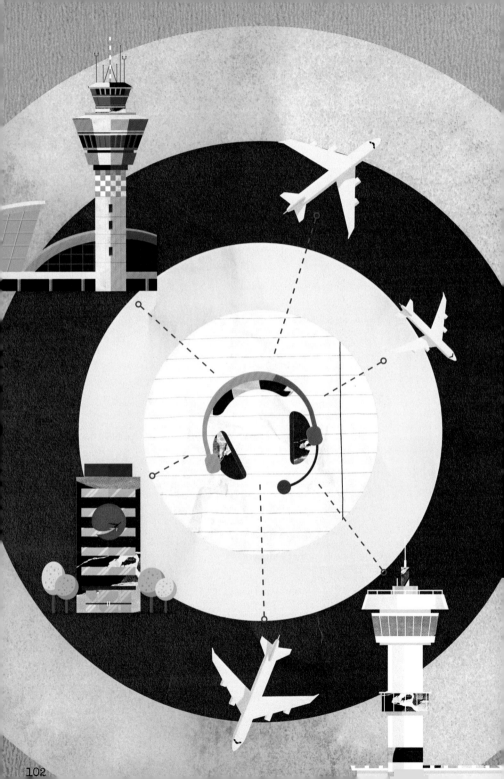

for the ramp that tell when and how we should push from the gate. Another set of controllers handles all the aircraft driving around on the **taxiways**, and a completely different set of controllers handles who can use the runway. After you leave the airport, you talk to a set of controllers that handles every airplane departing and arriving within twenty miles of the airport. And after *that*, there is a series of controllers you stay in contact with throughout the entire cruise portion of the flight. We even have frequencies so we can talk with our company, who monitors every flight that goes out. On top of all that, a pilot also pays attention to all the other airplanes on the radio so that we have a strong mental picture of who else is flying around us. (Remember, airplanes do not have brakes and they move fast. The best way to not run into another airplane is to never get close!)

24

DO PILOTS GET PAID A LOT?

This is the most surprising question I get asked! It is true that pilots must go through an incredible amount of education. It's also true that the skill of flying an airplane is unique and not something many people know how to do. There is a lot of testing and training that happens throughout your entire career.

Plus, every airplane is different. The basics of flying never change, but airplanes have lots of computers and systems. Learning one airplane does not mean you know other airplanes. As a rule, the bigger the airplane, the more computers and systems you'll have to know how to manage. That's why the career of a pilot will start with smaller airplanes and lead to bigger craft over time.

Your first job as a pilot will probably not pay well. Often, you get paid so little that you could make as much working at a fast food restaurant. This is because the company is hiring you to fly something small that does not have any passengers. They are also taking a risk, because you have not yet proven yourself competent. Over time, though, you can graduate to bigger planes and better jobs with more responsibility. With perseverance, you'll find that there are amazing, well-paying jobs for experienced pilots.

My first job was instructing other people who wanted to become pilots. This was in small airplanes with only two seats. I did that for almost 1,000 hours of flying. Then I went and flew an airplane that could take seven passengers; I was experienced enough to be trusted with that job. I was paid quite a bit more, too, because I was now a captain.

Then, I got a job as a first officer with an airline. This airplane was much bigger and much more complicated. I was also the first officer and not the captain. Captains get paid a lot more because they are the ones in charge, so I lost pay when I decided to become a first officer, but it was worth it to join the larger airline. Once I had enough experience as a first officer, I could apply to be a captain again, and that's what I am now.

GLOSSARY

airfoil: a shape that creates lift by moving air beneath the wing faster than above the wing

air traffic control: a group of trained professionals who coordinate the movements of aircraft around an airport

altitude: how high you are above the surface of the earth, usually measured in feet or meters above sea level

atmosphere: the blanket of air that surrounds the earth

bank: to roll an airplane slightly to the left or right

boarding pass: a passenger's ticket

cabin: the area of an airplane where passengers sit

captain: the pilot in charge of the flight

cargo: products or goods, including luggage, that are transported

climb: to move an airplane higher in the air

course: the direction an airplane is moving

crabbing: when an airplane flies at an angle to correct for wind

crew member: an individual who assists during a flight, like a flight attendant

crosswind landing: when an airplane banks slightly into the wind in order to land aligned with the runway

descend: to move an airplane lower in the air

drag: the force that pulls an airplane backward

embedded thunderstorm: a thunderstorm surrounded by ordinary clouds

first officer: the pilot who assists the

captain and consults on decisions

flight deck: the cockpit

frequency: a radio channel used for communication

fuselage: the main body of an airplane

gate: the area at an airport designated for arrivals or departures, often marked by a series of numbers or letters

global positioning system (GPS): a system that uses satellites to determine a specific location

gravity: the force that pushes an airplane down

instrumental landing procedure (IPS): a technological system used to land a plane when visibility is low

lift: the force that pushes an airplane up

pressurize: to increase the pressure of a space

radar: a system of radio waves used

to detect objects or weather in the surrounding area

reserve: when a pilot is on standby to fill in unexpectedly for another pilot

steep turn: when you bank the wings of a plane steeply and turn in a tight circle

taxiway: a striped, paved area used by aircraft moving around an airport

thrust: the force that pulls an airplane forward

touchdown: when the wheels of the airplane make contact with the runway during a landing maneuver

traffic collision avoidance system (TCAS): a computer system that allows aircraft to automatically communicate with each other when two planes detect that they are on a collision course

turbulence: when an airplane shakes, usually caused by moving air currents

ABOUT THE AUTHOR

Justin has been in love with aviation his entire life. Currently, he is a captain for Horizon Air, where he flies the DHC-8-400. As a pilot, he has transported people and cargo, explored exciting places like the Alaskan territories, and instructed others how to do the same. He studied aviation at Kansas State University. Justin lives with his amazing wife of thirteen years and their four children in Nampa, Idaho.

If you liked this book, please leave a review online at your favorite retailer. Honest reviews spread the word about Bushel & Peck—and help us make better books, too!

ABOUT BUSHEL & PECK BOOKS

Bushel & Peck Books is a children's publishing house with a special mission. Through our Book-for-Book Promise™, we donate one book to kids in need for every book we sell. Our beautiful books are given to kids through schools, libraries, local neighborhoods, shelters, nonprofits, and also to many selfless organizations that are working hard to make a difference. So thank you for purchasing this book! Because of you, another book will make its way into the hands of a child who needs it most.

NOMINATE A SCHOOL OR ORGANIZATION TO RECEIVE FREE BOOKS

Do you know a school, library, or organization that could use some free books for their kids? We'd love to help! Please fill out the nomination form on our website, and we'll do everything we can to make something happen.

www.bushelandpeckbooks.com/pages/
nominate-a-school-or-organization

Printed in the United States
by Baker & Taylor Publisher Services